MATH ON
SATURN

By Sarah Machajewski

Gareth Stevens
PUBLISHING

Please visit our website, www.garethstevens.com. For a free color catalog of all our high-quality books, call toll free 1-800-542-2595 or fax 1-877-542-2596.

Library of Congress Cataloging-in-Publication Data

Names: Machajewski, Sarah, author.
Title: Math on Saturn / Sarah Machajewski.
Description: New York : Gareth Stevens Publishing, [2017] | Series: Solve it!
  Math in space | Includes bibliographical references and index.
Identifiers: LCCN 2015051089 | ISBN 9781482449419 (pbk.) | ISBN 9781482449358 (library bound) | ISBN 9781482449259 (6 pack)
Subjects: LCSH: Saturn (Planet)–Juvenile literature. | Mathematics–Juvenile
  literature.
Classification: LCC QB671 .M33 2017 | DDC 523.46–dc23
LC record available at http://lccn.loc.gov/2015051089

First Edition

Published in 2017 by
Gareth Stevens Publishing
111 East 14th Street, Suite 349
New York, NY 10003

Designer: Laura Bowen
Editor: Therese Shea

Photo credits: Cover, p. 1 (Saturn) KPG_Payless/Shutterstock.com; cover, p. 1 (metal banner) Eky Studio/Shutterstock.com; cover, pp. 1–24 (striped banner) M. Stasy/Shutterstock.com; cover, pp. 1–24 (stars) angelinast/Shutterstock.com; cover, pp. 1–24 (math pattern) Marina Sun/Shutterstock.com; pp. 4–24 (text box) Paper Street Design/Shutterstock.com; p. 5 (main) Space Science Institute/Wikimedia Commons; pp. 5 (inset), 11, 13 (all), 15, 17, 19, 21 courtesy of NASA.com; p. 7 cigdem/Shutterstock.com; p. 9 (Saturn) Vadim Sadovski/Shutterstock.com; p. 9 (Earth) loskutnikov/Shutterstock.com.

Printed in the United States of America

CPSIA compliance information: Batch #CS16GS: For further information contact Gareth Stevens, New York, New York at 1-800-542-2595.

CONTENTS

Words in the glossary appear in **bold** type the first time they are used in the text.

BLASTOFF!

When darkness falls, the moon, stars, and other space objects light the night sky. Some planets are so bright we can see them with just our eyes. One of them is Saturn, called the "jewel" of our **solar system** for its beauty.

People have observed Saturn since ancient times. Recently, spacecraft have gotten close enough to the giant planet to take pictures and record **data**. Now, it's your turn to take a trip to Saturn. It's a long way from Earth, so your journey starts now!

YOUR MISSION

Math is an important tool for scientists who study space. In this book, math will help you complete important **missions** involving Saturn. Look for the upside-down answers to check your work. Are you ready to begin?

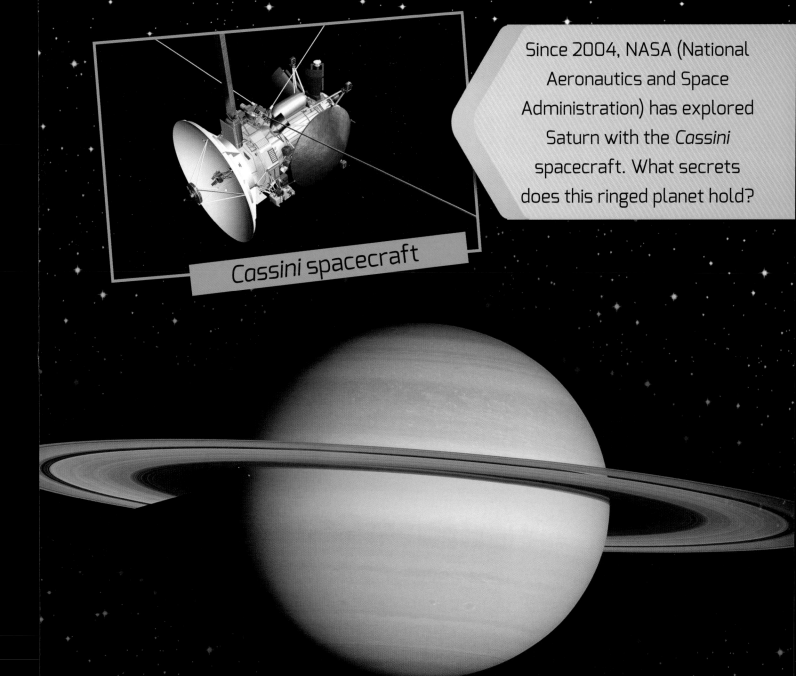

Cassini spacecraft

Since 2004, NASA (National Aeronautics and Space Administration) has explored Saturn with the *Cassini* spacecraft. What secrets does this ringed planet hold?

A LONG WAY FROM HOME

In ancient times, people could observe 5 planets in the night sky: Mercury, Venus, Mars, Jupiter, and Saturn. They didn't even need a **telescope**. Saturn was the farthest planet they could see. Considering that the closest Saturn gets to Earth is about 746 million miles (1.2 billion km), that's pretty amazing!

YOUR MISSION

Earth orbits, or goes around, the sun at an average distance of about 93 million miles. Saturn's average distance from the sun is about 794 million miles farther than this. What is the average distance between Saturn and the sun?

93 million + 794 million = ?

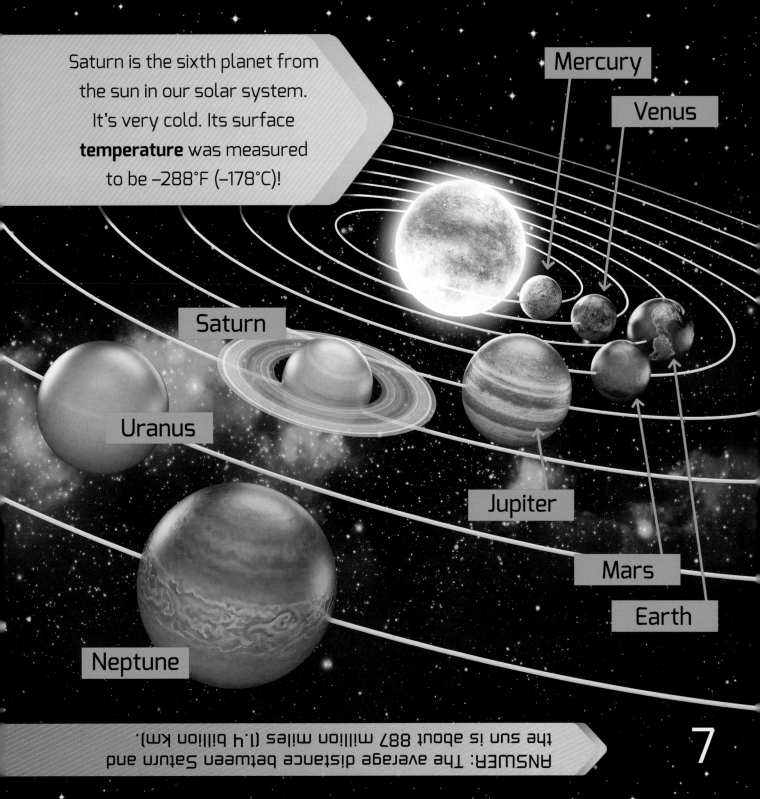

Saturn is the sixth planet from the sun in our solar system. It's very cold. Its surface **temperature** was measured to be −288°F (−178°C)!

Mercury

Venus

Saturn

Uranus

Jupiter

Mars

Earth

Neptune

ANSWER: The average distance between Saturn and the sun is about 887 million miles (1.4 billion km).

THE SECOND BIGGEST

Saturn is the second-largest planet in our solar system. Jupiter is the only planet that's bigger. Scientists have found out how big Saturn is by measuring its diameter. Diameter is the imaginary line that runs through the center of a planet, from one side to the other. Saturn's diameter at its **equator** is 74,898 miles (120,537 km).

YOUR MISSION

Jupiter is our solar system's biggest planet. Its diameter at its equator is 88,846 miles. How many more miles is Jupiter's diameter than Saturn's? Use the facts above to help you.

88,846 − 74,898 = ?

Saturn is so big that 9 Earths could fit across it in a straight line!

ANSWER: Jupiter's diameter is 13,948 more miles (22,447 km) than Saturn's.

ORBITING AND SPINNING

Compared to Earth, Saturn orbits the sun very slowly. One year on Saturn is more than 29 years on Earth! Saturn rotates, or spins, from east to west, just like Earth. However, it spins on its **axis** more quickly. One day on Saturn—one complete rotation—takes about 10 hours 33 minutes.

YOUR MISSION

A day on Earth—the amount of time it takes to spin once around its axis—is about 23 hours 56 minutes. How much shorter is a day on Saturn? Do 2 days on Saturn equal a day on Earth? Use the facts above to help you.

23 hours 56 minutes − 10 hours 33 minutes = ?

10 hours 33 minutes + 10 hours 33 minutes = ?

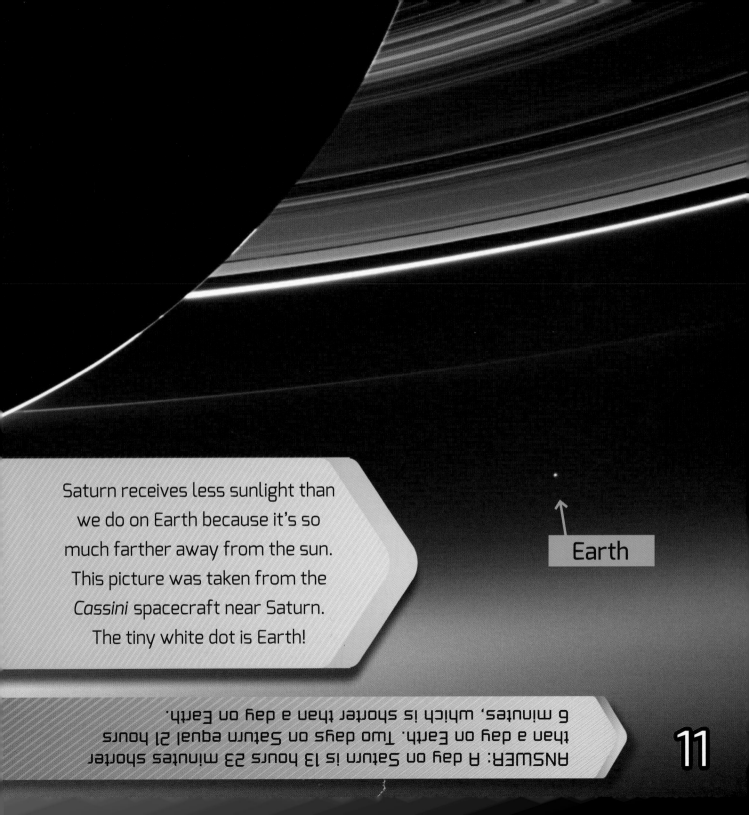

Saturn receives less sunlight than we do on Earth because it's so much farther away from the sun. This picture was taken from the *Cassini* spacecraft near Saturn. The tiny white dot is Earth!

Earth

ANSWER: A day on Saturn is 13 hours 23 minutes shorter than a day on Earth. Two days on Saturn equal 21 hours 6 minutes, which is shorter than a day on Earth.

A GAS GIANT

Even though Saturn is big, its surface isn't solid. Saturn is a gas giant, meaning its "surface" is made of clouds of gas. Its **atmosphere** is mostly hydrogen and helium. Saturn's **core** is made of heavier matter. Scientists think the core has a rocky **layer** the size of Earth or larger! It's surrounded by layers of liquid hydrogen.

YOUR MISSION

Even though it's an icy planet, Saturn's core is really hot! It may be about 21,150°F. The surface of the sun is thought to be around 10,000°F. Is Saturn's core temperature greater than (>), less than (<), or equal to (=) the sun's surface temperature?

21,150°F ? 10,000°F

Our solar system has four gas giant planets: Saturn, Jupiter, Neptune, and Uranus.

Neptune

Uranus

Jupiter

ANSWER: 21,150°F > 10,000°F. Saturn's core temperature is greater than the sun's surface temperature.

RINGS OF BEAUTY

Saturn is known for the beautiful rings that surround it. Saturn has 7 main rings. While some are hundreds of thousands of miles wide, they're all thin—probably only about 30 feet (9 m) thick in some areas. There are other faint rings that haven't been named yet, too.

YOUR MISSION

In order from the planet outward, Saturn's 7 main rings are named D, C, B, A, F, G, and E. The rings A, B, and C were discovered first. Represent these rings as a fraction of the total number of main rings.

$$\frac{A, B, C}{D, C, B, A, F, G, E} = \frac{?}{?}$$

In the 1600s, scientist Galileo Galilei observed Saturn through a telescope. He thought he was looking at a planet with handles or arms. These were Saturn's rings!

ANSWER: A, B, and C are 3 rings out of 7 rings, so the fraction is 3/7.

DISAPPEARING BEFORE OUR EYES

Saturn's rings are made of billions of pieces of ice and dust. Some pieces are very tiny, while others are the size of mountains! Scientists think the rings contain bits of asteroids, **comets**, or other space objects. Every 14 or 15 years, Saturn's rings seem to disappear. Actually, as Saturn orbits the sun, its rings turn so we can only see their edge.

YOUR MISSION

Look at the NASA chart on page 17, and use it to answer the questions. Which of Saturn's rings is the widest? Which is the narrowest?

16

SATURN'S RINGS

RING	WIDTH
D ring	7,500 kilometers
C ring	17,500 kilometers
B ring	25,500 kilometers
A ring	14,600 kilometers
F ring	30–500 kilometers
G ring	8,000 kilometers
E ring	300,000 kilometers

All the gas giants have rings, but Saturn's are the brightest and most beautiful. That's why it's the jewel of the solar system!

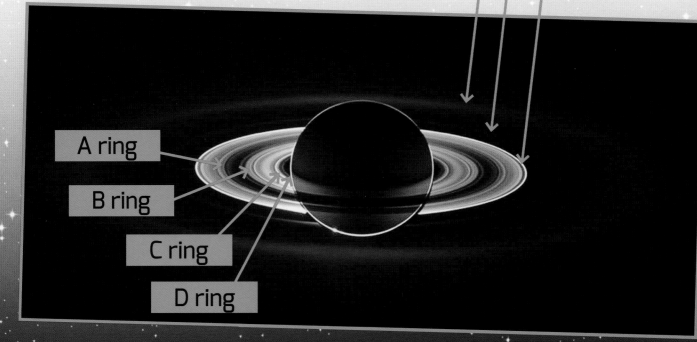

E ring

G ring

F ring

A ring

B ring

C ring

D ring

ANSWER: The E ring is the widest.
The F ring is the narrowest.

STORMS ON SATURN

Saturn is bright, icy—and stormy. Scientists think a huge storm hits Saturn about every 30 years. In 2010, the *Cassini* spacecraft recorded violent clouds of frozen water and gases that reached about 190,000 miles (305,775 km) across the planet.

YOUR MISSION

Saturn's winds have been measured to be as fast as 1,118 miles per hour. The fastest storm winds on Earth measured 253 miles per hour. How much faster are Saturn's winds than Earth's fastest winds?

$$1,118 - 253 = ?$$

Cassini captured images of Saturn's violent storms. In this image, the storm clouds are visible in the upper half of Saturn.

ANSWER: Saturn's fastest winds blow 865 miles (1,392 km) per hour faster than Earth's fastest winds.

THE MIGHTY MOONS OF SATURN

Saturn is surrounded by dozens of moons. Titan, the largest, has an Earthlike atmosphere. The moon Iapetus has one black side and one white side. Dione has a fractured, or broken, surface, while Mimas has huge craters. Many other moons have interesting features, too. What will scientists find out next about Saturn and its remarkable rings and moons?

YOUR MISSION

There were only 18 known moons orbiting Saturn when the *Cassini* spacecraft began its mission in 1997. So far, 44 more moons have been found. How many moons have been found around Saturn in all?

$$18 + 44 = ?$$

At 3,200 miles (5,150 km) across, Titan is Saturn's biggest moon and the second-biggest moon in our solar system. Here, Titan appears in its orbit around Saturn.

Titan

ANSWER: In all, 62 moons have been found around Saturn.

GLOSSARY

atmosphere: the mixture of gases that surround a planet

axis: an imaginary straight line around which a planet turns

comet: a space object made of ice and dust that has a long, glowing tail when it passes close to the sun

core: the central part of something

data: facts and figures

equator: an imaginary line around a planet that is the same distance from the north and south poles

layer: one thickness lying over or under another

mission: a job or task

solar system: the sun and all the space objects that orbit it, including the planets and their moons

telescope: a tool that makes faraway objects look bigger and closer

temperature: how hot or cold something is

FOR MORE INFORMATION

Books

Radomski, Kassandra. *The Secrets of Saturn*. North Mankato, MN: Capstone Press, 2016.

Squire, Ann O. *Planet Saturn*. New York, NY: Children's Press, 2014.

Steinkraus, Kyla. *Giant Gas Planets*. North Mankato, MN: Rourke Educational Media, 2015.

Websites

Cassini
saturn.jpl.nasa.gov/kids/
Learn more about Saturn through the eyes of the *Cassini* spacecraft.

Saturn: Overview
solarsystem.nasa.gov/planets/saturn
Read all about Saturn on this informative website.

Solar System 101
solarsystem.nasa.gov/kids/
Explore the solar system with NASA's fun, interactive tool!

INDEX